Bodhi's
Lemonade
5$

BODHI

The All American Lodge Dog

By Middleton Evans

A Ravenwood Press Book

RAVENWOOD
PRESS

Bodhi: The All American Lodge Dog

Photography by Middleton Evans

Ravenwood Press, Inc.
P.O. Box 496
Fallston, MD 21047-0496
Phone: 410-877-2432 / 800-807-1079
Fax: 410-877-2419
www.ravenwoodpress.com

Book Design and Text: Middleton Evans
Cover Design Consultant: Patrick Reid O'Brien
Contributing photographers: Kristie Evans, Andrew Hall, Tina Llewellyn
Costuming Consultant: Connie Pribyl
Typography and Graphic Production: Elizabeth Davidson
Film Scanning and Digital Processing: Andrew Hall
Photoshop Compositing (10 Images): Rob Ronda
Printing by Pacifica Communications
Bodhi Interview by Aurora Kief

Library of Congress Control Number: 2007922389

Contents:

Dedication

To Bodhi... I am eternally grateful for our friendship of the past five years. Your enthusiastic greetings lift my spirits every time I visit the Lodge. I cannot thank you enough for humoring me on all of my wild picture concepts; you never let me down, not even once. I hope the shoots were as fun for you as they were for me. Your playfulness and passion for life has inspired my creative energies to seek new horizons. I hope that I have served you well with your mission of bringing joy to the world.

I also wish to dedicate this book to Mike Dreisbach and Jan Russell, Bodhi's humans, for having the courage to chase your dream and open the Savage River Lodge against all odds. You both work impossible hours, always with a smile, to ensure that the Lodge stays open 365 days a year. With wide arms you welcome the weary of the world, myself included, to rest, dine and celebrate nature within the divine sanctuary that is Mount Aetna. You have also provided a wonderful home for Bodhi, who shares his gratitude every time a Lodge guest checks in. Your impeccable hospitality has brightened the lives of countless guests seeking comfort from all the stress of modern life. Well done, Mike, Jan and Bodhi!

11

12

Introduction

This is a story of Amazing Grace. A dog so loves his human companions that he delivers an Oscar performance on every set, somehow knowing that these photo shoots and subsequent calendars help his parents' lodge business by bringing joy to the world. Like many stories, it starts quietly with the planting of a seed. That it would mature into a mighty oak, none of us saw it coming except, of course, God.

I love dogs. Ever since I was a kid, I couldn't resist petting any friendly dog that crossed my path, even at the risk of an asthma attack, which often ensued. When twelve, I put milk out for a stray lab mix who happened upon our house. "Sam" ended up sticking around for ten years and readily became my best friend. Little wonder that I grew up to be a wildlife photographer. In the fall of 2001 I was hired by Nita Settina of the Maryland Forest & Park Service to photograph Mt. Aetna for a new trail guide. She told of a jovial yellow lab that I would meet at Savage River Lodge. On that initial visit Bodhi posed like a champ with Jodie, the front desk manager, for some fun hiking shots. What a good sport, I thought, knowing how difficult it is for my dogs to sit still for any picture! Little did I know what had just started. A few hours later I sat down with Mike and Jan, the Lodge owners, and conversed freely as kindred spirits enthralled with the natural world. I autographed a copy of *Maryland's Great Outdoors* for them. Soon after, we talked about the possibility of a coffee table book about the Lodge and Mt. Aetna's natural splendor. The seed had just been planted.

Within a few weeks, I was back at Savage putting down roots. My shots for Nita were completed, but I felt the gravitational pull of Mt. Aetna and just went with it. I investigated several beaver ponds along Mudlick Run. It's hard to lay your eyes on these primarily nocturnal animals, but their signs are everywhere... the phrase "appetite for destruction" comes to mind. The woods along Mudlick Run have tremendous character, with unusual trees capturing my attention at every bend. Early in my career I was preoccupied with showy subjects like butterflies and birds. As my connection to nature has matured I find the plant kingdom equally fascinating, and there is no lack of spirit in the Savage woodlands. It is a magic mountain, perfectly suited for a sage like Bodhi.

Over the next year I would make about six visits to Savage to begin work on the *Savage Beauty* book. I didn't realize it then, but I was laying a foundation for this collection by learning about the mountain and the surrounding area, including scenic spots where I would later pose Bodhi. Mike and I had numerous conversations about the local wildlife. A number of elusive predators pass through Mt. Aetna, including fisher, bobcat, coyote, black bear, mink, and fox, both red and gray. Immeasurable time and faith would be required to encounter them all, but this is my intention. Your prayers are welcome.

Intermingling with these forest phantoms are plenty of watchable wildlife species just waiting to be discovered. I have hiked the trails of Mt. Aetna all four seasons and there are many highlights worth noting. First and foremost are the deer, well entrenched on the mountaintop by the Lodge. They are fed corn during the lean winter months and quite amenable to close-up viewing any time of year. I'll never forget discovering a newborn fawn bedded down a few feet from the Lodge parking lot. I rushed back to the cabin for my camera and returned for some exquisite photo ops. Most hikes will also turn up chipmunks scurrying across the forest floor and red squirrels chattering from evergreen perches. Both hit high pitch notes easily mistaken for birdsong.

This little slice of Appalachian Eden is a birder's paradise. Nearly one hundred species have been identified to date. Hit the trails in high season and you are likely to encounter the scarlet blaze of a passing tanager, the thumping drum of a lonely grouse, the dazzling acrobatics of nectaring hummingbirds, the throaty gurgle of distant ravens, the kamikaze splash of a hungry kingfisher, the whimsical fluting of serenading thrushes, and hammering of logs by industrious woodpeckers. From raptors to game birds, warblers to waterbirds, Savage is a feathered tree garden. I'll never forget my first life sighting of a male rose-breasted grosbeak, visiting a feeder by the Lodge. It was a little angel with a scarlet heart.

If small creatures pique your interest, then the warmer months will not disappoint. Butterflies fill the meadows, especially near the river bridge. Thistles, milkweeds and cardinal flowers entice spectacular fritillaries, swallowtails and monarchs. Little winged jewels also abound. I will always cherish the discovery of a mated pair of American coppers in dense grass. Oddly enough a flying butterfly led my eyes to this needle in a haystack, as if by divine guidance. At night moths can-

vas the landscape... you may wake up to find a luminescent luna moth anchored to your screen door, provided the porch light was left on overnight. Frogs, toads and salamanders inhabit the wetlands, but a confirmed sighting may cost you some wet sneakers. Turtles and snakes are rare surprises, well worth the wait, depending on your fear factor.

Against this backdrop of robust nature viewing, the greatest treasure of Savage - Bodhi Lodge Dog - was right before my eyes the whole time. Little did I know what adventure the next four years would bring. Sensing this *Savage Beauty* book was going to take years to complete, Mike got the idea one fine day for a Bodhi calendar to launch in 2004. At first I drew a blank when approached; I had no experience doing posed shots of pets and wondered how to fill a calendar without being predictable and repetitive. The eternal optimist Mike rattled off a few ideas... in hunting attire with a shotgun and decoys, on a trout fishing trip, having a "Bodhi Beer," and so on. Always up for a challenge, I signed on for the project. In February 2003, I took my first Bodhi theme picture as he howled on Mike's snowmobile. Brainstorming on the topic, I came up with a few

good ideas myself... campfire marshmallows, stalking a turkey, and riding in a canoe. In six months we completed twelve scenes, and the 2004 calendar was a big hit with Lodge guests. I immediately started daydreaming about the next edition, and had no problem coming up with another twelve ideas for Bodhi scenes that would surely put smiles on faces and joy in hearts. What an honor it has been to work with Bodhi. He has no training or practice for our shoots; he just shows up for work every day and somehow knows that we need a magic moment on film, which he graciously provides. As Bodhi easily handled challenges, my picture ideas emboldened. Bodhi interacting with a box turtle... now that was a long shot. Against all odds, I found a wild male relocated to a private garden the year prior, and it did not clam up when handled! For sure the box will snap shut when a dog appears, I thought. But this was Bodhi Lodge Dog with the Midas touch and he and the turtle did just fine for our photo shoot. Bodhi lowered his head for a sniff, affecting a partial retreat of the turtle's neck, but they still maintained eye contact. There are moments when life is purely sublime.

In the spring of 2006, while finishing up work on the fourth calendar, Mike suggested that I make a book about Bodhi for national release. Once again, I pulled back, thinking of all of the challenges ahead. One other thing... Mike wanted the book out for April 2007, less than a year away; I usually spend about four years on a book! He was really shooting for the moon, but I signed on, trusting that if it was meant to be, God would show me how to pull it together.

Upon reviewing the 50 photo shoots already completed over the past four years, I realized that I needed more material. I am a big dreamer and knew that if I was going to make a Bodhi book, my best work was still ahead of me. Prayers went out for new ideas, and picture concepts flooded back like a river... kissing a frog, a pool party, riding in an antique convertible, an old-fashioned soda fountain, chasing deer, Davy Crockett's cabin, and Noah's Ark. That one I immediately dismissed as too ambitious, but I told Mike and Jan about it anyway. A few days later they were driving along Highway 81 (north of Hagerstown) and alas, there was a beautiful Ark parked at Nevin's Furniture. Back on the list, I investigated the ark, secured permission from the owner, and proceeded to collect stuffed animals with Kristie's help over the next two months for an unforgettable image. From August through December 2006 we completed another 50 shoots, accomplishing in four months what I had done with Bodhi in the past four years. This I can only chalk up to God's amazing grace. Bodhi was an old dog with bad hips, yet he still gave his all to bring my ideas to life. We became the best of friends and shared many amazing moments.

While conceptualizing the design and content of this book, I got the idea to have an animal communicator interview Bodhi. I had recently purchased Kim Sheridan's *Animals and*

the Afterlife as a gift for a friend who recently lost her black lab. After reading parts of the book, I sensed that animal communication was legitimate, and started my search for a local commu-

nicator. While conducting a nature photography workshop in Baltimore that August, I met Aurora Kief, who clearly had a special connection to the natural world. I asked her to interview Bodhi, to which she kindly agreed. An explanation of her techniques appears on page 186. At first glance it may seem absurd that a dog could be interviewed, but I find it far more improbable that an untrained dog could intuitively bring my photographic visions to life time and again. I'd love to hear an evolutionist try to explain that one!

Bodhi sees it as his job to bring smiles and joy to the heavy hearts of Lodge guests. Now, with this book, he takes his mission across the country and around the globe. As a caretaker of three dogs, I can testify to the unflinching love, loyalty and good nature of man's best friend. Overflowing with gratitude, I can only thank God for creating these furry wonders who add so much comfort to our lives. Imagine a world where humans love each other the way our dogs love us -- it must be close to Heaven. Until then, we gladly embrace the constant love offered by our furry angels...

Middleton Evans

17

Chapter One
Once Upon A Time

Once Upon a Time

"What's in a name?" This famous Shakespearian quote is a question we've come to understand completely through our beloved yellow lab who entered our lives as a family pet, but became so much more. He became an actual family member, spiritual companion, business partner and the goodwill ambassador known as Bodhi Lodge Dog.

The naming of this energetic ball of fur back in 1995 was the first indication of his uniqueness. Mike's daughter, Arrity, had selected the name "Bodhi" from a movie character portrayed by Patrick Swayze. Jan quickly reminded Arrity that the chosen name was very spiritual, and in Buddhism was a name intended for an enlightened being. We've since realized his name was not a happenstance; he is like an old being from another time who was sent to us for a reason.

Our newest family member, however, was not always so perfect. He most definitely was 110% yellow lab puppy – he chewed, ripped, tore, and tormented everything. Arrity had assured us that she was going to play a very active role in the training and caring of this wonderful ball of enthusiasm. But, as with most young people, the responsibilities of pet care, pet walking, and pet training soon went way down on her daily list of priorities. He was even banned from her room after it was discovered that he had eaten her Victoria's Secret underwear.

He flunked out of "kindergarten" three times. Obedience wasn't in his vocabulary at an early age. When he transitioned from a choke collar to a pinch collar (it was the only things that would slow him down) he was a star pupil and finally graduated from obedience class. On Bodhi's first day of

> He flunked out of "kindergarten" three times. Obedience wasn't in his vocabulary at an early age.

class (on our fourth attempt), the trainer asked if he could use him as an example. Of course he was much better behaved, because he was much older than his classmates. The trainer took him to the middle of the circle of dogs and instructed him to sit and stay, which he did perfectly (we were beaming with pride). He then backed away from Bodhi and said "come". Bodhi came and sat in front of him. "Good Boy" said the trainer as he tossed a morsel to him as a reward. Bodhi caught it and promptly spit it out. Was that rude or what? After a moment he went to the morsel and sniffed it, picked it up again and promptly spit it out. One more try and he decided that he would eat it. Everyone was of course chuckling and curious as to why he didn't eat his treat. The trainer was just as curious until we found out that the treat was a piece of hot dog and Bodhi had never eaten meat in his life. The next time he did the sit-stay-come he was thrilled to get his treat.

This "obedience school graduate" still needed someone to teach him how to peacefully coexist in our home, which at this time had become the office and planning center for the development of the Savage River Lodge. Most of our time and energy was being devoted to this project that we knew was our purpose in life as well as our legacy. The last thing we needed in our lives was this rambunctious yellow lab puppy.

Fortunately for Bodhi, Jan, whose deep spirituality came from her Native American ancestry as well as her knowledge of Christianity and Buddhism, assumed the role of trainer and mentor. She developed a "plan of attack" which included

lengthy walks every morning, afternoon, and evening. Fortunately for the family, Bodhi became less of a "holy terror." He was spending hours exercising and playing with his teacher and spiritual mentor and we began to feel that this creature was not just a pet, he was something very unusual and different.

Not only was Bodhi smart and becoming a better family member, he also had quite a sense of humor. Some neighbors had installed electric fences to confine their pets to their own yards. We consulted our veterinarian, Dr. Franklin, about such a system for Bodhi. However, he told us that Bodhi was very smart and could be taught where his boundaries were without the aid of a fence. After several weeks of us saying, "Stay in your yard," Bodhi knew his limits. He also knew how to drive Petey, the neighbor's Dalmatian, crazy. Bodhi would go to the edge of the yard and stick his head across the fence and touch noses with Petey. Tails would be wagging then Bodhi would back up and coax Petey to come towards him. Zap, Petey would bounce back from the electric shock, and continue to do it over and over again.

In the fall of 1998, construction began on the Savage River Lodge and Bodhi, who had grown up in suburbia, enjoyed the many trips to the Maryland Mountains. He loved the freedom of taking a hike without the constraint of a leash and the joy of chasing chipmunks, but didn't understand what happened to them when they dashed into a hole in the ground. More often than not, there would have to be a quick bath in the river before his car ride home, as he was very fond of rolling in something that had been dead for a long time.

...he was very fond of rolling in something that had been dead for a long time.

We also learned of his compassionate and caring disposition in the mountains. While working on building our first cabin in the woods, Mike slipped from a ladder and found himself hanging upside down from a floor joist. He wasn't injured, but couldn't quite figure out how he was going to extricate himself from his precarious position. Jan ran to his aid to find Bodhi by his side, licking his face which was 8 inches from the ground. When our laughter finally subsided we were able to get Mike upright while Bodhi looked on, knowing that he had "saved his life."

By the spring of 1999, it was time to move to the mountains to finish construction of the Lodge.

At this time Bodhi's transition from puppy to Lodge Dog began. It was as if the first five years of his life had been a training mission to "enlighten" his human partners and prepare them for a journey that involved a new sense of spirituality, his, as well as their own.

Our new log home on the property became the Lodge's construction office with contractors coming and going daily. Bodhi loved all the activity and attention and decided to make himself the construction supervisor. He would sneak off each day at lunchtime to visit the construction crew. When we realized that he was gone we would head to the construction site. However, seeing us coming, he would cleverly sneak back through the woods – only to be found lying on the front porch when we returned.

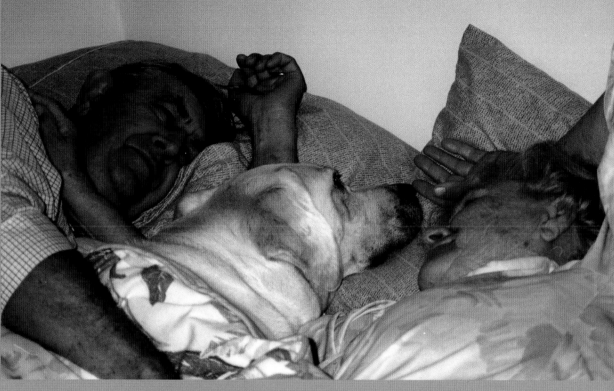

As with all projects, there were delays. The Lodge's dining room and kitchen weren't quite finished for the first guests. They were treated instead to a "bed and breakfast" experience where breakfast was served in our home. Still very much the puppy, Bodhi enthusiastically greeted these guests by inappropriately jumping on them to say "hello" and would cry when he was made to stay in the office rather than under their breakfast table. He knew then that he had a very important job as "ambassador" and was responsible for making the guests happy.

As we prepared to officially open the Savage River Lodge we were absolutely terrified about bringing this "wild creature" into the mix of guests who were coming to the Lodge for a peaceful and serene experience. We worried what would happen in the Lodge and how our guests would

He knew then that he had a very important job as "ambassador" and was responsible for making the guests happy.

react. Would Bodhi continue to jump on everyone who walked through the door and sit under the tables in the restaurant? We were amazed that as soon as the Lodge opened, Bodhi's jumping on people stopped, and he only had to be told once that he was not allowed in the restaurant.

Bodhi quickly became the head of guest services and, as seen on his business cards, was officially titled "Bodhi Lodge Dog." He assumed the responsibility of welcoming all guests (humans and pets). He would lie on the front porch just waiting to greet them or act as a guide on the surrounding trails of the Savage River Forest. Bodhi would guide for hours, if necessary, bringing the hikers and their pets safely back to the Lodge. Guests often commented that Bodhi would cut the trip short if it was near lunch or dinner time; he didn't want to miss a meal.

25

When the Lodge started hosting business groups with attendees who had agenda packed meetings, Bodhi became responsible for a new level of service. After welcoming the group he would follow the guests upstairs into the meeting room and patiently wait to dutifully clean up the crumbs that fell from their plates. Or he would sleep comfortably in the middle of the room where his snoring would interrupt some very tense moments. But the service he enjoyed the most during these meetings was to allow a shoeless attendee to give him a bare – footed belly rub while he rested under the table.

One morning during a business meeting, the event coordinator came to us a bit annoyed that the coffee break refreshments hadn't been brought to them. We checked with the kitchen staff and they assured us that the muffins had been taken upstairs prior to the scheduled break time. The mystery was solved after noticing the blueberry stained teeth and muffin breath on the Lodge Dog. He had stolen and eaten a dozen blueberry muffins from the coffee break table!

It was established that Bodhi's vocation was that of Lodge Dog, but his avocation is super–model. He loves to have his picture taken. Often a guest will come into the office to ask if someone can take a photograph of the family by the fireplace. Bodhi will practically knock everyone down to get there first and position himself in the front row of the smiling faces. He has appeared in more than a few "family photos."

In 2002, the state of Maryland commissioned a photographer, Middleton Evans, to take photographs of the forest surrounding the Savage River Lodge. Middleton not only took pictures of the forest area, but he also took a few pictures of Bodhi. Our "Diva in a Dog Suit" was born and a true friendship of kindred spirits began.

The idea of a "Bodhi Lodge Dog Calendar" was conceived, and together, Middleton and Bodhi began their project of photographing Bodhi and his friends in various poses and settings

The mystery was solved after noticing the blueberry stained teeth and muffin breath on the Lodge Dog.

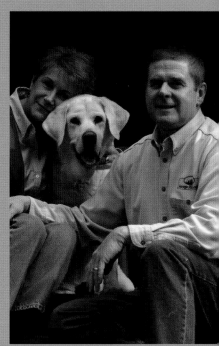

in and around the Lodge. Middleton was successful in capturing the true spirit of Bodhi, and their collaboration has helped to bolster Bodhi's reputation as not only the Lodge Dog but a year–round goodwill ambassador.

True to his name, Bodhi, now twelve years old, continues to "enlighten" everyone he encounters here at the Savage River Lodge.

Jan Russell and Mike Dreisbach,

Jan Russell & Michael Dreisbach

Chapter Two
A Day
In The Life

"My workday starts at 6:45am. Dad usually drives me in the official limousine to the Lodge. I like to bring Tigger along for the ride. My first job is to clean up crumbs on the dining deck from last night's dinner. I love sloppy eaters... the bacon bleu burger ROCKS!"

"I spend a lot of my mornings in the office. I like to keep Mom and Miss Tina company. They work long hours taking reservations and planning fun activities for our guests. I love it when guests come into the office and play with me. Mom and Dad put silly signs in the office about me being a guard dog."

"By mid-morning, I need to get out of the office for some fresh mountain air. Sometimes I sit on the porch and count butterflies passing by. When dog guests check in, I give them a good sniff to let them know who's boss around here. When pretty girls check in, I get excited and play soccer with my red ball."

"Sometimes people eat lunch on the porch and I score big, even though my mom put signs everywhere about not feeding me. Sweet potato fries are my favorite. I also like to kiss my human friends when they rub my tummy and back after lunch."

"I get a salad for lunch every day at noon sharp. I love tomatoes, cucumbers, and carrots. I won't eat celery or mushrooms... I tried them once and I just can't do it. FedEx stops by the Lodge around noon each day. When my friend Bill is on duty, he always puts treats out for me. The DHL guy doesn't give me anything, so I don't wag my tail for him. After eating, I like to snooze in the shade under the awning."

"Most guests arrive after my noon nap and I welcome them to the Lodge with a big smile. Most come from the city and are really stressed out... some even put smoking sticks in their mouth. Guests think it is really cute when I follow them into the lobby. Brittany takes me in the limo to show guests their cabins and I show their dogs my favorite potty trees."

43

"When I get really smelly, Dad takes me down to the river to give me a good washing. We also play fetch with a stick and I like to splash around. Sometimes when I'm in the water I don't mind when the pretty trout swim between my legs, but when I accidentally step on a crayfish, that hurts! Even though they're little those buggers can bite hard. After the swim, they rub tug-of-war towels all over my body and it makes my arthritis feel better."

"This past year, my media friend has been taking lots of pictures of me. I get a bath before we work together. I don't know what a picture is, all I know is that he points the black box with the circle glass at me and presses down a little button. When I give a good pose, he smiles and laughs a lot, pressing on the button so many times that I lose count. He just about wore me out with this lemonade gig."

"At night I go back to my house with my family. Grandma Bea likes to massage my ears, while Dad thinks I'm a foot warmer. He stares at this really big piece of paper for a long time. Some nights I fart a lot and the girls just laugh and laugh... it is one of my favorite games. Being a lodge dog really wears me out and I am asleep by 9pm. Ever since Doc Franklin put me on Rimadyl for my arthritis, I sleep like a baby, dreaming of all those bacon bleu crumbs to clean up next morning."

49

Chapter Three
A Walk Down
Memory Lane

It's A Small World

While on our first official family vacation to North Carolina's Outer Banks, one day we decided to catch the ferry and head over to Ocracoke Island for the day. We did all the usual tourist things, like visit the lighthouse, get the boys' picture at Teach's Hole, and eat at Howard's Pub. While walking through town Dennis noticed a decoy shop that he wanted to check out, so we stopped in. We got to talking with the owner of the store about a particular antique, a seafood crate from Southern Seafood Company in Baltimore. While we were chatting a man standing in line turned to me and asked what part of Maryland we were from, so I told him and asked the same question of him. When he said he was from Cumberland I immediately said, "Oh one of our favorite vacation spots is out there... Savage River Lodge." The man said, "Oh, then you must know Bodhi the Lodge Dog!" We both laughed! Here we were on this tiny little island off the shores of North Carolina and we found common ground through Bodhi! It turns out that he lives not far from the Lodge and goes over for dinner with his wife.

– *Tricia and Dennis Wilson*

52

The Panhandler

When the Lodge was under construction Bodhi saw himself as the construction supervisor. He would sneak out of the office at his house and wander through the woods at noon to check on the contractors. He would go from crew to crew, stopping to have lunch with whomever would invite him. He had quite the variety of foods: donuts, sandwiches and potato chips (if the bag wasn't open, he'd just eat the chips – bag and all!). He returned back to the office one afternoon with an unpeeled hard boiled egg in his mouth. He was quite proud of his thievery. He didn't know what it was or what to do with it and didn't want to give it up. After having it in his mouth for probably half an hour he finally dropped it, cracking the shell and exposing the delicious treat. He devoured it quickly, shell and all.
– *Jan Russell and Mike Dreisbach*

Bodhi's Fan Club

The funniest things happen at the marketplace. At Belvedere Square in Baltimore (200 miles from Garrett County), I was handing a complimentary Bodhi calendar to my friend, Allyson, when the woman behind me in line blurted, "Bodhi! You know Bodhi?" You would have thought she had just caught Elvis buying a latte. She joyfully recounted her visits to the Lodge and times of loving-up on Bodhi.
–*Kristie Evans*

Off to the Races

Bodhi had way too much energy when he was a puppy. The only thing that slowed him down was several long walks a day and some Frisbee catching. It was chaos when it rained and none of this happened. We finally came up with a way to wear him down. We started by chasing him around the house, which wore us out, but not him. Mike would stand at one end of the house and Jan at the other, one would call him and he would race their direction, then the other. It finally came to be "here he comes – there he goes". He loves the big porch at the Lodge. When he got excited he would run to find a toy then race from one end of the porch to the other with guests cheering him on with "here he comes – there he goes." As he's gotten older he doesn't run the whole length of the porch, but the sparkle in his eyes lets you know that the puppy is still in there wanting to.
– *Jan Russell and Mike Dreisbach*

Runs Like Clockwork

When Bodhi was a pup and before the Lodge was built, the family would "camp" in the cabin in the front meadow. One fine summer day while on one of these "camping trips," Mike's daughter, Nicole, and Bodhi went for a hike. The two hadn't been gone long when we glanced out the window and saw Bodhi running towards the cabin. He raced up the steps and barked at the door, wanting to come in. What could possibly be wrong? Was it a "Timmy and Lassie" moment? Was there trouble in the woods? No, it was 12:00pm. After we fed him his lunch, he ran back to the door and barked. We let him out and off he ran to the woods to catch up with Nicole on her hike.
– *Jan Russell and Mike Dreisbach*

Into the Woods

When I think about Bodhi I fondly recall the walks that we have taken. Bodhi is eager to share the trail with everyone. No matter how much you try to trick him and take another path, he will go ahead of you. On one hike he was especially excited to find something particularly smelly and proceeded to roll in it. My husband, Tom, had to give Bodhi a bath upon reaching the Lodge even before he could have his traditional salad lunch.
– *Joanne Roland*

Say, "Cheese!"

He is truly a "diva in a dog suit" and has always loved to have his picture taken, even before his first calendar was published. Often guests will come to the office and ask if someone can take a photo of their group. By the time someone can come from behind the counter and get to the photo location, Bodhi has gotten up off of his bed and is sitting in the front row of the group waiting for his picture to be taken.
– *Jan Russell and Mike Dreisbach*

55

Splish Splash

Bodhi loves swimming and fetch. When he was a youngster he had a good friend, Dozier (a rottweiler), who had a swimming pool. Dozier would invite Bodhi for a swim party every week. Bodhi would wait for the "fetcher" toy to be thrown in the water and would swim to get it, while Dozier would wait patiently on the side of the pool hoping the "fetcher" would float to him so he could grab it. If Bodhi got to it first, Dozier would go to the steps and swim out to meet Bodhi. They would then swim side by side to the steps and get out. Then do it all over again, and again, and again.

– *Jan Russell and Mike Dreisbach*

Great Expectations

One of my favorite memories of Bodhi was when we had traveled from California for a visit. Early one moring, Jan told Bodhi that "MeeMaw and PeePaw are coming to see you." We were expected late in the day. As the morning turned into early afternoon Bodhi got excited and kept running from Jan's office to the window in the living room. She kept telling him "they aren't going to be here until late," but he continued to race back and forth and bark which finally forced her to get up and go to the window. "See, I told you they weren't here". He paced at the front door and she looked down the street and saw our truck – 10 houses away. He sensed our arrival 10-15 minutes before we arrived. We were thrilled to see him run out the door to greet us with a toy in his mouth as usual. This time it was a special toy, the one we had given him when we left six months earlier. He is the best "grand dog" in the world.

– *Bea Reed*

Bodhi and the Bank

Bodhi has loved going to the bank ever since he was a puppy. The drive-thru tellers would, of course, give him dog biscuits. They would talk to him and he would "Speak" until they sent a biscuit out to him. If we went into the lobby, the Branch Manager would ask about him. If we said that he was in the car, they would insist that we go out and get Bodhi and bring him in to visit. He very quickly found his way to the tellers at the drive-thru and where they kept the biscuits. Jan's dad used to tell the story of going to the bank to cash a check. He had left his wallet in the car and started to go out and get it. The teller stopped him and said "You don't need to get it, we know who you are. You're Bodhi's grandfather."

– *Bea Reed*

Bed Hopping

When Bodhi was a couple of years old he would go to bed at his regular time and wait for me to come home... usually later than I should. As soon as he would hear the front door open, he would sneak out of Dad and Jan's bedroom doing a "low crawl" on his belly. As soon as he would get to the hall he would race in my room and ask to be allowed in bed, and we snuggled all night long.

– *Tasha Dreisbach*

We Love You Bodhi

We first met Bodhi when my husband, John, and I visited
Savage River Lodge, to write a story for my *Cumberland Times-
News* weekly wellness column. We seemed to have a mutual and
instant love for each other. Subsequently, we spent several
weeks and weekends "personal retreating" to this marvelous
oasis only 15 miles from our home. Our bond with Bodhi grew
to be different than with any other animal we have ever known.
The first time we picked up Bodhi so he could take us for a
walk, I remember Mike saying, "You know you have the mil-
lion dollar dog!!" Wow!! We began to realize that Bodhi is a
huge part of the Lodge signature and even had his own web
page on their website! Once we decided which way we were
heading to the river to play, Bodhi bounded ahead. Sometimes
we could see him; other times, as he rounded a bend, he was fur-
ther ahead. When we got to the river, Bodhi and John played
"fetch" until John became tired. We wanted to return a different
way, so I called Bodhi's name and, for the first time, got very
close to his face and I felt like our souls met. "Bodhi," I said,
"John has discovered a different way home. When we get to the
red trail, we are going to go off to the right. Also, it would be
good if you stay nearer to us, not getting so far ahead." As he
sat, I said this to him several times. He cocked his head, as
though to reassure me that he "got it." This gesture has continued whenever we spend time and communicate with him. When

we got to the "Y" in the trail that day, Bodhi bounded up the
red trail, just a few feet to the right, paused and looked at me,
soul to soul, as if to say, "Did I get it right?" He stayed with us,
only a few feet ahead and never again went out of sight. His
knowledge of the trails is perfect. There is no doubt that he
could lead anyone "home to the Lodge" if they got lost.

Lunchtime is important for Bodhi and he is used to eating a freshly prepared salad each day. We were walking a mile or
so from the Lodge one day and he began to act a bit strange,
running fast and seeming to want to return home quickly,
which was unusual. Suffice to say, we had forgotten about his
lunch date and he turned totally happy when we arrived for his
"a bit late reservation!" The only time Bodhi and we had a dis-
agreement was when he found a very old deer carcass, a good
distance away from the trail. We called and called; nothing could
lure him; even the doggy treats that we carried lacked their usual
power! Finally, John walked across the little ridge to the site and
discovered why Bodhi wouldn't return. We returned to the
Lodge immediately, with Bodhi in tow, and helped Jan and
Mike give Bodhi a bath in the parking lot. It was a lot of fun.

One time when we enjoyed a week's vacation, celebrating our 30th wedding anniversary, Bodhi accompanied us on
hikes everyday. We were staying in Cabin #11. I decided to test
our soul-to-soul communication once again. As we were returning the first day, I asked Bodhi to sit and we looked at each
other, heart to heart again. "Bodhi, we're staying in Cabin #11.
Please take us to Cabin #11." As we walked, he veered off the
trail near this cabin and went to the porch steps, turning as he
did on the first hike, as if to say, "Right again, Amy and John?"
That entire week, he brought us "home" to Cabin #11 and
bounded up the stairs. It was awesome! In the beginning of our
relationship, Bodhi would whimper outside the dining room
when we went in to eat supper. Then we started to reassure
him, "Bodhi, we're going in for dinner. We'll see you later. It's
okay." With hugs, pats and that ever present eye-to-eye communication, his understanding always seemed complete.

Both John and I are Reiki and Bodhi loves to lie beside
us and allow this universal energy to flow through him. It has
been especially helpful, it seems, for his hips and when he has
been hurt while romping in the woods. He settles completely
and we know he understands the healing power of our love. We

have always been amazed at his joy when we arrive. We may have discovered why. We knew a person who communicates with pets and Jan agreed that bringing her for a visit might be fun. When Sandi asked Bodhi who his littermates were, he rolled his eyes, looking around the room and said to her, "Well, who do you think these people are?" Jan, Mike, John and I were present. He does, indeed, think that he is a human! Bodhi's love is immense. One time, when I brought flowers to someone at the Lodge, as a token of my sadness, Bodhi calmly lay beside me and later, as I cried, surrounded me with his love. His usual bois-terousness was gone; he knew a good friend was hurting and his calmness and outpouring of love were remarkable. Bodhi defi-nitely takes his job as Lodge Dog seriously. On walks through the cabin area, he knows which cabins have canine visitors and he always runs up onto the porch, to check and see if everything is okay. We have never met a more amazing and influential dog than Bodhi. His intuition and love oozes out of his heart and soul like the warmth from the muffins he delivers to the cabins each morning. We love you, Bodhi!!

– Amy and John Shuman

Chapter Four
Diva In
A Dog Suit

"I work long hours, and wear many hats, but it's not a bad life being the Lodge Dog. My first job was construction foreman... let me tell you, good help is hard to find up here in the mountains. Sometimes I start up the engine on the snow plow while Dad makes the coffee. I recently started my own line of dog biscuits. Only Chef Steve and I know the recipe... these things sell like hot cakes!"

"Hit the gas, Mike, we've got three miles of trail to groom and I haven't even started on the hot chocolate! Cool your jets, Jan, there's lots of children down there and we don't want an accident on the first day of winter break! Safety comes first on Bodhi's Mountain."

"Back in the old days we had to hunt if we wanted to eat, but now food comes in a bag from the Wal-Mart. We still go hunting for old-time's sake, but my pop misses most of the time, and that's o.k. by me 'cause the meat is too gamey for my taste."

"Once upon a time, my great grandpaw and Davy were the best hunting team this side of the Mississippi. The only time I got really scared, children, was when that big mean cougar stalked me, but Davy got 'em right between the eyes just before he was gonna pounce on old Bodhi Crockett. Yep, those were the days."

"Don't worry, Bambi, Mommy is coming back soon, and I'll make sure that the coyotes don't get you. Our Lodge guests just love seeing the little fawns running around the mountain! As for you, Newton, you'd better crawl under a rock, 'cause that hawk is looking for lunch!"

"Throw it back? You've got to be kidding me! I just don't understand you humans. It took me two hours to catch the biggest, baddest trout in the whole river, and the last thing I'm gonna do is release him. Besides, I haven't had Trout Almondine in months!"

"That's far enough, Bodhi! Why don't you go and smell the pretty flowers in the valley. I can't have the Lodge Dog breaking a leg on slippery rocks just because a great big bull-frog hopped into the falls. Trust me, it DOES NOT taste like chicken!"

"Make your move, John Boy, it's getting hot out there and my lemonade stand needs tending to." Meanwhile, back at the ranch… "Just a sip, Junior, up here in the mountains we add a little moonshine to our lemonade. We can't have you stumbling along to the soap box derby with Reverend Tom being the judge this year."

"I just love the change in seasons. My favorite time of the year is winter, when we have to gather lots of firewood to keep our guests warm. I am never going to retire to Florida... I'd just melt down there with this fur coat on all the time."

"Ahh autumn, I don't know who has more fun playing in the leaves, the neighbors' kids or me. 'Bury Bodhi' is the game they like to play. And it's also the time of year that I, "Big Daddy Bo," get to go trick-or-treating with my canine crew. Knocking on doors and getting treats – now that's fun for kids and dogs."

"On holidays my humans love to dress me up in silly costumes and take lots of pictures, smiling and laughing the whole time. The next day they trudge off to work with a frown and get stressed out again... I don't understand you humans. In my world every day is a holiday, and I smile from sunup to sundown."

"Pass the chips and salsa, Pedro, and an extra margarita for the señorita. The Lodge serves Bodhi Beer, and it's o.k., but this Cinco de Mayo stuff really packs a wallop! Tomorrow morning is going to be rough, but I always leave some Tylenol on the nightstand."

"Hey Rudolf, get me a crowbar. We've got to get that cap off the chimney if I'm ever going to make these deliveries! And Blitzen, remind me next year to get a bigger sleigh, like the one at Pleasant Valley where my folks used to take me for Santa School. You should've seen that giant reindeer... it was as big as a horse!"

"I just love having company. Good friends are just about as important as good oxygen to breathe! In the fall I invite my bird dog friends, Tucker and Max, to the Lodge and we watch geese and ducks migrating south. Winters can be lonely, so I build snowmen and we dress alike. We mostly just talk about the winter wonderland atmosphere here at the Lodge."

89

"Good Morning, America! How about some farm fresh eggs and a flower for the lady? Yesterday, Dad and I went to the market. The tomatoes didn't smell right, so we didn't buy any, but farmer John's peppers were perfect... they are really good in a salad or omelette."

"Having this plain white fur makes me envious of you, Miss Monarch, with your dazzling, jewel-like wings. You are the most exquisite creature I've ever seen. Sometimes in my dreams I'm a bumblebee pollinating all the flowers just like you. But I know I'll have to wait for Heaven to get my permanent wings."

Charlotte's Web

"Back off, Bodhi, it took me all night to weave this web, and if your nose gets stuck the whole thing will fall apart."

"Don't worry, Miss Charlotte, I wouldn't dream of spoiling your handiwork, I'm just amazed that I can see myself in all the little dew drops – you have created a masterpiece!"

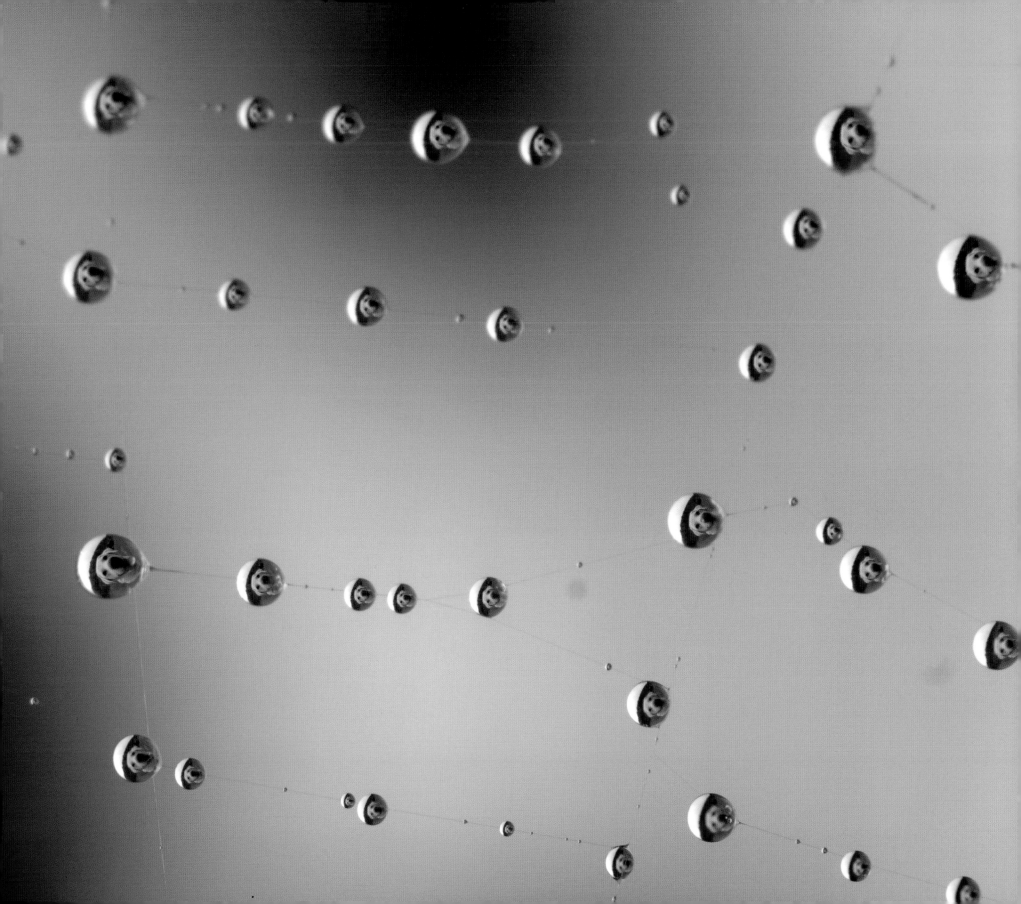

"We've got so many maples up here on Bodhi's Mountain that I figured we could cut costs and make our own syrup. When Dad agreed, I volunteered for the quality control job, and the Savage River Lodge label doesn't go on until I've tasted every batch of liquid gold."

"Ye fish of the great northern ice lake have made a noble sacrifice for our head chef to whip up another culinary masterpiece for our guests. Hurry up and catch a fish, Luke, I'm cold and tired, having caught all 22 fish myself. Today I have the Midas Touch."

"Make that three scoops plus sprinkles, Michelle. I just had my check-up and Doc Franklin says my cholesterol is the lowest it's been in six years. Naturally we had to celebrate the good news at the corner soda fountain... and that's all I have to say about that."

"Bodhi, you can't bark at the auctioneer just because he has a funny voice. Now I have to tie you up at the hitching post with the Amish horses. I'll bid on some produce for the restaurant and pick you up in half an hour."

"I've won so many ribbons at dog shows that I've lost count. We train down at the reservoir a few times each month. This one duck I fetch must be mute, because he never talks back to me. Another part of my practice routine that I love is jumpin' logs; it makes me feel like I'm flying. Just call me Air Bodhi."

"I didn't do it, Sheriff Andy, I would never tinkle on your boots 'cause that would be disrespecting an officer of the law. My mom can't bear the thought of me locked up all by myself! I'll sniff down that dastardly canine culprit if you just give me the chance. I have a sneakin' suspicion that Marky Max was involved, and I know just where to find him."

Field and Stream

"I know that I'm not supposed to scare off the geese, but this is ridiculous! I prefer to set up decoys on the river and then snuggle up with Dad in the blind until the ducks fly in. Good thing for the birds that my dad misses a lot, but you didn't hear it from me."

The Tortoise and the Terrapin

"How many times do I have to tell you, Bodhi, we took terrapin soup off the menu years ago. Put him back in the river, now. Think of him as a friend, like Baxter the box turtle that you keep meeting on the orange trail. Remember when you promised Baxter never to tell the chef about him?"

"Oh boy, Chef Steve, that bird is roasted to perfection. I'll take a drumstick and a wing, then pass it on down. I stalked old Tom for three hours down in the hollow. He was dancing and strutting up a storm, then BAM!! Miss Betty felled our Thanksgiving bird with just one shot... and that's all I have to say about that."

"I'm the chief game warden around here, and I run a tight ship. I told Bart the beaver that he could chew up as many trees as he'd like along Bucktooth Lake, but never come up to our cabins and chew on those logs or I would have to arrest him for malicious munching of private property."

"No hot-dogging on the trail, Nordic Man, I've already made three rescues and that's plenty for one day. Now I don't want to be late for my noon salad! Last spring ol' Dave held me up 'cause he wanted to smell all the pretty laurels, and that was our last hike together."

"Do you hear the bells? Do you hear them ringing? I found this dazed skier who'd been lost for two days, and I saved his life. The papers did a big story about me, and I finally got my wings! I always knew that I lived in Heaven."

"Times just aren't like they used to be. I liked it better in the old days when the pace of life was much slower and the ride was as much fun as the destination. These young whipper-snappers today rush to the mall, rush to soccer practice, rush off to Target... For the love of God, where has the romance gone?"

"One day I got a call from my friends at the Violetville VFD. They needed a "fire dog" to ride with them in the Independence Day Parade. I was such a "hit" that I've been asked to be the Grand Marshall next year. My daddy always said, 'Life's like a box of biscuits.'"

"I come from a long line of service dogs. My grandma, Bodhette, was the famous Café Dog at the Café Hon in Hampden, where Baltimore hons like to shop – and gladly mug for the camera. Her signature red cat-eyed glasses and blonde beehive were a hit with the patrons at the restaurant, as was the Bodhette Burger, loaded with bacon and bleu cheese crumbles. And yes, according to Grandma Bodhette – blondes really do have more fun!"

"Maryland is a great state for retrievers and blue crabs. As a matter of fact, my cousin, the Chesapeake Bay Retriever, is the official state dog; and crabbing is one of Maryland's most treasured industries. One time in Annapolis the legislators proposed putting new limits on the crab catch and I, Barrister Bodhi, went to bat for my watermen friends. I lobbied at the State House for expanded fisheries 'cause we need to keep those crabs piled high on the tables all across the state."

THE CRAB IS IN

OLD BAY.
SEASONING
For Seafood,
Poultry, Salads,
Meats
Same great taste
for over 60 years
NET WT 6 OZ   170 g

I'M CUTE NOT CRABBY!

I ♥ CRABS
©USC

M A R Y L A N D

"Hey, Bodhi, mister fancy Lodge Dog with your own calendar line. I'm Peyton, the new Motel Dog at the Super 8 along the National Pike. I'm gunning for your record of 4,297 guests greeted with a smile. I've brought my top lieutenant, Tommy, to work you over a bit, 'cause I'm the new kid on the block, and I'm making waves... let's RUMBLE!"

"Ever have one of those days when you feel like a big, bad wolf? Well, I did, the time my folks took me for a dog sled ride and these three Huskies gave me a heck of a time! This one named Rascal got right in my face and told me to be quiet while I was there. Now is that any way to treat a guest? I wouldn't think of acting that way when my wolfhound friend, Gandolf, comes for a visit to the Lodge."

"I just love being a star. I get to do the COOLEST things, like hanging out with my friends at Yellow Snow Dog Adventures... mush, mush! Please take it slow through the Yukon Pass 'cause I want to take in the view of those majestic mountains. God Bless America."

"I, Secret Agent Bodhi, have gone undercover on several occasions in Lancaster County to solve crimes. The first crime scene was over at Yoder's Farm where several of their goats were missing. I set up "Operation Scarecrow" to solve that mystery. Another caper was catching the reviled Pumpkin Bandit of Wilson's Lane. While disguised as a giant pumpkin I sprang into action and was able to pin down the bandit with my pearly whites."

135

"Hey Bodhi, over there in the maple grove, I see three spectacled bipeds in adult plumage. That rose-breasted male is in peak breeding color, and he's attracted two hens!"

"Yep, Hootie, that's my mom and her friends; they count all the little birdies in the trees, and then they go eat chicken in the restaurant... go figure!"

"I get to meet so many babes as the Lodge Dog...it's even better than being a lifeguard. One day this "hottie", Jenny, was dating Marky Max until she caught a whiff of someone else's Liz Claybone on him and she dumped that two-timing rat right then and there. Well, I wasted no time inviting that hot strawberry blonde for dinner at the Lodge and I even broke out my ace in the howl - Tommy Holediigger cologne. And the rest is, as they say – history. What happens at the Lodge, stays at the Lodge!!"

"Later that evening, after my memorable dinner with Jenny, I fell asleep and dreamt of my new "flame." I was leading her down a secret path in the Fairy Forest where alas, we found our wings and kissed amidst all the forest spirits. When I awoke the next morning I had to return to the "real world" and resume my job as a trail guide where I was called upon to identify some lovely butterfly specimens."

Bone Appetit

"As a young pup I was fond of big soup bones and would protect them with all the ferocity of a hungry wolf on a deer kill. Somewhere along my journey meat no longer tasted good, and I became a vegetarian. My dreams took a dramatic turn, exchanging the rush of chasing rabbits and squirrels for the peace of tending my garden and counting butterflies."

"Entertainment at the Lodge is pretty old-fashioned. We don't have those fancy things like TV's and DVD's, but we do enjoy our most popular slide show, "Diva in a Dog Suit". But my personal favorite is "Bodhi and the Beast." Another old-fashioned Lodge activity is campfires. I just have to look all sad and hungry and I can score lots of marshmallows – campfires rock!"

145

"You must take this call, Bodhi, you are in grave danger and must meet your tribe at #112 Maple Lane immediately. They can't complete their mission without Porky Pig to guide them safely along the dark streets of Frostburg."

"Oh look, a flock of robins has flown in to sing me Happy Birthday... isn't life grand! On my tenth birthday I wished for peace and goodwill for all. Hey there lonely bullfrog, come out and join the party. If you let me plant one on your cheek, we can both be princes for a day!"

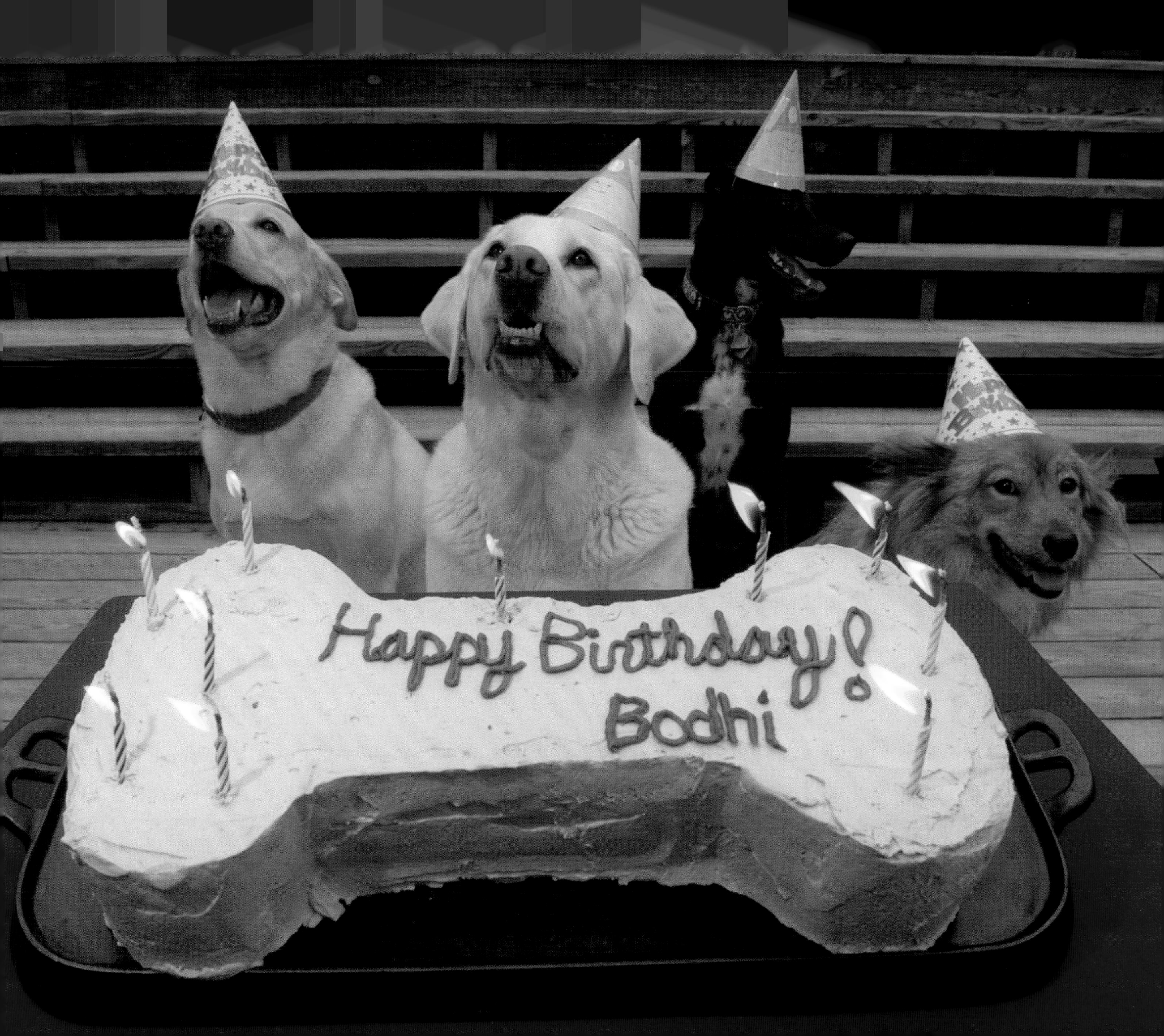
Happy Birthday!
Bodhi

"Hey Noah, that was a great idea to put stripes on my back; now the lonely zebra mare thinks she has a mate like everyone else, and she's jumping for joy. We'd better load up this ark now, 'cause storm clouds are brewing on the horizon. You did stock up on Bodhi Biscuits and blueberry muffins, right? I think that it's going to be a long ride..."

151

"Be still, animal spirits of turtle and pony tribes, I mean you no harm. I am Bodhi Lodge Dog, and I bring good news. In Heaven we will play forever in flower-filled meadows and you will not have to worry about getting run over by a car or having somebody sit on your back. Humans have taken over this world, but in the next we are all equal and safe."

Chapter Five

Straight from the Lab's Mouth

Bodhi's Interview with Aurora Kief

AURORA: Tell us about your name "Bodhi."

BODHI: The name Bodhi means Bodhisattva to my people (Mike & Jan), but it has a closer meaning for me with the Bodhi Tree. Animals & nature are always connected and intertwined. I carry the Spirit of the Bodhi Tree with me.

AURORA: Who are you and what is your purpose?

BODHI: I am a benevolent, loving being who comes into the planet to serve by unconditional love. I am also a teacher. My purpose is to help Mike and Jan however I can and also to help others unburden themselves. Sometimes they will speak with me about their troubles because there is no one else they can trust.

AURORA: What gives you the most joy?

BODHI: The most joy I get is running and playing fetch. I also like to go in water, if it's not too deep, while Mike fishes.

AURORA: What do you like the best about your position as Lodge Dog?

BODHI: I like all of the attention I get as Lodge Dog. It makes me happy that people treat me well and they laugh and smile with me.

AURORA: Do you have any words of wisdom for Mike and Jan?

BODHI: Keep loving me and caring for me. Keep loving each other - especially when I leave you. Protect the land you are care-taking. Be at peace with all living beings. Let the Greater Beings take care of us.

AURORA: Any advice about improvements to the Lodge?

BODHI: Lodge improvements - a water conservation system is a good idea. More fans. Some solar panels are a good idea.

AURORA: You seem to love having your picture taken. Why is that?

BODHI: I love to have my picture taken, because it makes people happy. That's part of my job. I know I am doing a good job when they laugh. I am a patient being. I have learned what Middleton requires to be happy with me and I want to do a good job with Middleton, because I like being with him. I don't know what a camera is, but I respond to what Middleton wants me to do, because he is a good person with good intentions for us.

AURORA: Why has your calendar been such a big hit?
BODHI: Because I touch people's hearts through the pictures and make them laugh. It reminds them of fun.

AURORA: Are you aware that we are making a book about you?
BODHI: No, the book is about all of us - and the lodge - and our friends.

AURORA: Do you like the title Bodhi: The All American Lodge Dog?
BODHI: Yes, it is a good title.

AURORA: Can you advise us on how many books to print?
BODHI: About 250 for the first printing.

AURORA: What would you like to say to your friend and camera man Middleton?
BODHI: You are my dear friend. You know how to talk with me - not like Aurora, but through a shared understanding of our work together. You are more than a camera man. You are an artist, Middleton. The art is your love and faith and goodness put into our work for the world to share. I love you. Thank you for your respect of my kind and finding ways for us to be with one another. I just want to say "Thanks".

AURORA: Why are labs the most popular breed of dog in America?
BODHI: Labs are the most popular breed of dog in America, because we love being with people and having fun with them. Labs are kind hearted beings - benevolent.

AURORA: What is the difference between a dog and a wolf?
BODHI: Dogs and wolves are the same tribe. Wolves are more natural - living by instinct and listening to the land. Dogs are more tamed by humans. In times long ago wolves slept with the people and protected them. It was people who caused the separation.

AURORA: Why do dogs roll in smelly animal poop on the trails?
BODHI: For the sheer joy of removing human scent from their coats. It also has vitamins in it for the hair and skin.

AURORA: Dogs seem to live for the joy in each moment. Why is it so hard for people to do this?

BODHI: Dogs teach this, because it is their nature. It is only hard for some people, others have mastered it.

AURORA: What words of advice do you have for people to learn how to 'live in the moment'?

BODHI: (Bodhi asked me to explain this – because he couldn't understand what I was asking him – he had no concept of not living in the moment). He said to be yourself. If you like something enjoy it, play, and bark loud! If you don't like something, make sure you put your head down, tell them with your body – "I don't like this. I don't want to do this." — Bodhi had a hard time with this, since he always lives in the moment.

AURORA: Are you aware of all the forest creatures and spirits that live on your mountain? Do you ever communicate with them? Is there a connection between all living creatures?

BODHI: I am aware of all of them. The spirit of the mountain brings me peace. I communicate with all the creatures and tree spirits and the elementals in certain places. There is a connection, especially on our mountain. Many spirits are free here, myself included. This brings a great peace and joy to our land and the creatures. This is a natural community where all are intertwined.

AURORA: Why are dogs so much more loyal than people?

BODHI: Dogs know their jobs and serve where they are sent - unconditionally.

AURORA: What can you tell us about God?

BODHI: God is part of it all. The animals, the plants, the waters, the peoples.

AURORA: Are you aware of what a mess people have made of the world?

BODHI: People have not made a mess of the world. It is a place where all beings come to learn, grow, interact.

AURORA: What do you know of death? What about heaven?

BODHI: Death is a passage back to spirit form. Birth is a passage into physical form. It is in the moment. Heaven is a feeling of the heart that people put a picture with.

AURORA: What has it been like to get old?
BODHI: It is peaceful. I spend more time in the "other world" now. I will be leaving soon. I am preparing my people and myself. I want my parting to be with the same joy that I brought here.

AURORA: Can you tell me about your recent operation?
BODHI: I felt sharp pain and then I was In Between and being held by my Keepers until it was time to go back.

AURORA: Did you have a choice about whether you were going to die?
BODHI: No, I knew that I was going to come back after being repaired. When I came back, my Keepers lowered me in through my head until I was steady. I felt sore in my belly and very, very tired. And then I saw my people, Mike and Jan, and I knew that I was going home and would be okay soon.

AURORA: Are you ready to pick and train your successor?
BODHI: There will be a successor. It won't be me. It is a girl Lab. She is my color. She has a brother that wants to live here, also. They are twins. They are from Tennessee. I will go with my people to find them, if they want me to.

AURORA: Will people be reunited with their beloved pets in heaven?
BODHI: For a brief visit. Then animals and people go to separate places until they ask for one another again.

AURORA: How is it that some people like Aurora can actually have a conversation with a dog and others can't?
BODHI: Because Aurora's heart is open to the love that is shared by all living beings. Anyone can have a conversation from heart to heart. Others converse from the place of Universal Mind and can communicate with all beings (forms of telepathy).

AURORA: Do you remember a special little girl that visits the Lodge?
BODHI: Yes, I remember her. She has braids. She can speak with me in her head. I like her, because she and I can communicate, truly. She knows.

AURORA: What do you dream about?
BODHI: Running, playing in water, chasing birds. I sometimes dream of the other worlds I have known. I dream of my people some. Sometimes in my dreams, I am healed by them. I dream a lot about playing and I shake.

AURORA: What is your favorite memory with Mike and Jan in this life?
BODHI: When I was a puppy and got in a muddy mess & they carried me in, I got a bath and they played with me with the drying towels. That was great fun and I still get happy when I remember that. One other favorite was when they started to get my bandanas. I like them. They are like costumes for me.

AURORA: What about the "Ghost" at the lodge?
BODHI: It is a man. I can see him. He's not harmful to us, but he scares some of the people. He is an old trapper who used to have a cabin there. He wants to stay with us. He likes it here. I bark or whine at him when he 'talks' to me, but nobody can see or hear him, except me - and that person who came and could 'sense' him. He laughs when I bark at him.

AURORA: Why do you bark so fiercely at the friendly deer that live on your mountain?
BODHI: Because part of my animal instinct is trained as a hunter to identify other animals. I do that by barking.

AURORA: Are you aware that people hunt deer on the mountain? How do you feel about that?
BODHI: I am aware. I feel it is part of the cycles of nature. I don't think it is good or bad, just part of my life here.

AURORA: What would you say to all the people who have come to the Lodge?

BODHI: There have been so many. The excitement, the playing, the petting, the greetings, and some that I didn't trust and had to watch (some were bitter and mean and would hurt me, so I "warned" them to stay away). I could have helped them, but they just wanted to hurt me like they were hurt, so I stayed away from them. Others were glad to see me again and again. I healed their stress when they laughed, or walked, or petted me. Some of my lodge friends had not played for a long time and I gave them that time of play, again. It helped with the stress so they could go back to their lives in a more peaceful way. Tell some of them that I knew them before in other lifetimes, so there was a great reunion, rejoicing when our eyes met. Tell them, Middleton, my press man, "Thanks for the memories."

AURORA: Is there anything else, Bodhi, you would like to say?

BODHI: We have come a long way with understanding one another. I am a healer. Communication with me and my kind is becoming more understood. It is like learning another language. When we learn the language of interspecies communication, we can truly say "Bodhi speaks" and we listen.

161

Chapter Six

Walk on the
Wild Side

The 700-acre Mt. Aetna Tract of Savage River State Forest features two picturesque waterways – Mudlick Run (center) and the Savage River (far left) – that are easily viewed from the Red Loop Trail. A native brook trout stream, Mudlick has seen plenty of beaver activity in recent years, as evidenced by this dam overflowing with melting snow. These same river banks are graced by blooming rhododendron (far left) in mid-summer. Smaller feeder streams (above) cascade down the mountains and empty into the Savage River, as does Mudlick Run just downstream from the river bridge.

Crowning Mt. Aetna is a 45-acre parcel privately owned by the Savage River Lodge, the dream-come-true getaway created and managed by Mike Dreisbach and Jan Russell. The 10,000-square foot Lodge, opened for business in 2000, features an award-winning gourmet restaurant and bar, an outstanding wine list, gift shop, library, conference room and cozy nooks where one can curl up with a book or chat with friends. Bodhi loves to hang out on the front porch and greet guests with a good wag of his tail.

Just a short walk from the Lodge, eighteen private luxury cabins await guests and their canine companions. There is no lack of creature comforts; all cabins feature a cozy sleeping loft, spacious soaking tub and shower, separate vanities, refrigerator and gas log fireplace. Each morning fresh muffins and juice are left in a basket on the porch. Even when fully occupied, an air of utter tranquility permeates the grounds, except for singing birds and chattering squirrels.

The Enchanted Forest

Hardwood forests of maple, oak and poplar dominate the landscape of Mt. Aetna. Several acres of planted pine and larch near the Lodge help to diversify the habitat for a variety of wildlife. Many species of wildflowers festoon the woodlands, meadows and stream banks from April through October. Pictured here are (counter clockwise from lower right) pink lady's slipper, green coneflower, bluets and jewelweed. These Appalachian forests are among the most diverse ecosystems in all of North America.

Hit the Trails

Fifteen miles of trail are open to the public for year-round adventures. With an elevation range from 2,285 to 2,600 feet, the loop trail gives hikers and birders quite a workout, though easier trails by the cabins can be selected for moderate exercise. Winters are a splendid time to visit Savage; the Lodge offers a Nordic Ski Shop to accommodate cross-country skiing and snowshoeing. The unique geography of Garrett County attracts lots of snowfall, with a climate more reminiscent of New England than the mid-Atlantic region.

The woodlands of Mt. Aetna harbor a great variety of mammals, though most are nocturnal and highly elusive. One is guaranteed, however, to see white-tailed deer (right) on virtually every trip, as they frequent the grassy areas by the Lodge and cabins. Within the Lodge's private 45 acres they are safe from hunting and stick close by this sanctuary. Black bear (left) commonly pass through the area; sightings of sows with cubs are not uncommon. The handiwork of beavers (above) is hard to miss along Mudlick Run, where a healthy colony has pillaged the hardwoods for several years running.

With nearly 100 species identified to date, Savage River State Forest is a birdwatcher's paradise. Spring and summer offer the best viewing by far, as many varieties nest here, including a dozen kinds of warblers, thrushes, vireos, sparrows, woodpeckers, raptors, ducks, game birds and the ubiquitous American Robin (above). The Common Raven (left) is also a Savage fixture; in recent years a pair has nested in pines by the Lodge. The Ruby-throated Hummingbird (far left) is easily viewed at feeders by the Lodge, but there's plenty of wild nectar along the trails.

A great variety of bugs and herptiles call Savage home. Butterflies are easily viewed feasting on wildflowers in summer meadows. Here a black swallowtail and great spangled fritillary (far left) share a thistle blossom. A mated pair of American coppers (preceding pages) is a rare treasure. Moths are more secretive, though porch lights may attract special overnight visitors like this polythemus moth (below). Beaver ponds and vernal pools make perfect breeding sites for amphibians like the spring peeper (left), more easily heard than seen. The eastern spotted newt is prolific here; the terrestrial juveniles (top), called red efts, glow like jack-o-lanterns as they crawl across the forest floor.

"The name Bodhi means Bodhisattva to my people (Mike & Jan), but it has a closer meaning for me with the Bodhi Tree. Animals & nature are always connected and intertwined. I carry the Spirit of the Bodhi Tree with me."

— *Bodhi*

Resources

Antietam Recreation *(wild west show)*
9745 Garis Shop Road
Hagerstown, Maryland 21740
301-797-3733
www.antietamrecreation.com

Café Hon *(Elvis & friends)*
1002 West 36th Street
Baltimore, Maryland 21211
410-243-1230
http://cafehon.ezsitemaster.com

Hometown Girl *(soda fountain)*
1001 West 36th Street
Baltimore, Maryland 21211
410-662-4438
www.celebratebaltimore.com

Nevin's Furniture *(Noah's Ark)*
15021 Molly Pitcher Highway
Greencastle, PA
717-597-7047
www.nevinsfurniture.com

Pleasant Valley Dream Rides *(sleigh ride)*
16889 Pleasant Valley Road
Oakland, Maryland 21550
301-334-1688
www.pleasantvalleydreamrides.com

Violetville V.F.D. *(fire truck)*
4000 Benson Avenue
Baltimore, Maryland 21227
410-242-3131
(Donations are welcome)

Western Maryland Scenic Railroad
13 Canal Street
Cumberland, Maryland 21502
301-759-4400 / 800-TRAIN-50
www.wmsr.com

Wilson's General Store
14921 Rufus Wilson Road
Clear Spring, Maryland 21722
301-582-4718

Yellow Snow Dog Sled Adventures
Oakland, Maryland 21550
301-616-4996
www.yellowsnowadventures.com

Technical Notes

I started this project with film cameras – Nikon F100 and F5 models. In 2004 I made a slow transition to digital and now use the Nikon D2H and D2X models. Approximately one quarter of this collection was shot on film – Kodak E100 VS and Fuji Provia and Velvia films. Digital images were recorded on Lexar Compact-flash cards as JPEG fine files. Photographs selected for publication were "cleaned-up" in Photoshop and saved as TIF files. In addition to dust spot removal and cropping, images were adjusted for contrast, saturation, color balance, shadow detail and sharpness in a few cases. Seven images in this collection had major Photoshop work, compositing a main scene with Bodhi and secondary elements from another image. Bodhi and the deer were photographed at the exact same location, just not at the same time, as is in the case with the flying swallowtail butterflies. Sixteen Ark animals were added to the foreground, as we did not have enough doubles to fill the entire scene. His two canine trick-or-treaters would not sit still with the diva, so we shot them separately. The hand-held terrapin was added later as Bodhi declined to hold it in his mouth. The bullfrog with Prince Bodhi was enlarged a bit, though Bodhi did offer a "kiss" when first presented with this captured bullfrog. Another six photos had minor cosmetic surgery, like the addition of a cornpipe that was too small for Scarecrow Bodhi to hold in his mouth, though he certainly tried. The remaining shots in the book are single exposures, including Charlotte's Web. A few words on Aurora Kief's interview are in order. She did not visit Bodhi in person, but instead contacted him in meditation. If Bodhi was available to speak, his face would appear. Upon asking Bodhi a question, Aurora "hears" Bodhi through a mental connection whereby his language is instantly translated into our language. Questions were not necessarily answered with words; sometimes Bodhi would project an image for Aurora to interpret. Needless to say how this all works is a mystery, even to the communicator... some call it a spiritual gift. If you are interested in contacting Ms. Kief, please write to her at P.O. Box 331, Highland, MD 20777.

Acknowledgements

First and foremost, I thank God for giving me this lifetime to experience so much beauty and wonder in your Creation. The gift of your Son, Jesus, has transformed my life after many years of navigating without a compass. When I dreamed of a magical Bodhi book, You showed me how. This project has truly been a team effort, with many individuals contributing their talents and time out of a mutual love for Bodhi. To Mike and Jan, I offer a world of thanks for all of your efforts towards my long list of Bodhi shoots. To Aurora Kief, you are gracious beyond measure, translating Bodhi's wisdom, love and grace. To Kristie Evans, your encouragement from the beginning was vital to this project. You did a fine job behind the camera for the Ark, Lemonade and Leprechaun shoots, and also found a number of key props... I couldn't have done it without you. To Andrew and Jennifer Hall, you are consummate professionals, helping out with lighting, modeling and shooting (page 13, 68, 76). Thanks for a superb job on the slide scanning and digital clean-up. To Patrick Reid O'Brien, thanks for consulting, yet again, on the cover design. To Elizabeth Davidson, congratulations for putting up with me on another book project with many changes to the layouts. Thanks for coaching me through the design process to keep things clean. To Rob Ronda, you did a great job compositing several key scenes. To Connie Pribyl, a standing ovation for assembling so many costumes for Bodhi and the American Gothic look. For stellar venues and props, I wish to thank Steve Heacock (birds of prey), John Harvey (barnyard tractors), Ernest Schrock (rustic cabin), Jacob Yoder & Family (garden & goats), Mary and Andy Rotz (western show), Bob Pearsall and the Rausch Family (antique fire truck), Ms. Frances Horst (general store), Wayne Robertson (railroad conductor), Denise Whiting (nostalgic café), Jeff Matthews (Noah's Ark), Mary Pat Andrea and Michelle Squirewell (soda fountain), Ray and Rachel Miller (sleigh ride), Robin Turner (St. Bernard collar), Kim Trickett (dog sled ride), Mitchell Cathell (antique car), the Llewellyn Family (Halloween kids and Photos page 17, 161), Ron Boyer and Liz McDowell (beaver pond), the Wall Family (terrapin), Joe Ondek (frontier clothing), Tracey Brotemarkle (toy dogs), Tricia and Dennis Wilson (decoys), and Sherri Pavol (photo page 54 top). Valuable contributions to this book were also made by Karen Reckner, Kathy Hose, Patty Manown Mash, Brittany Harman. Bill Colbert, Amy and John Shuman, Steve Brown, Dave and Annie Lemarie, Greg Carter, Bea Reed, Arrity Dreisbach, Andy Deakin, the Farrell Family, Joanne and Tom Roland, Tom Dembeck, Lee Haile, Luke Mongrain and a number of Lodge guests whose names went unrecorded. Thank you all for contributing so graciously, a powerful testimony to the love that Bodhi fosters. Each of you has left your permanent fingerprint on this story of Amazing Grace.

Savage River Lodge
A Dream Come True

The Savage River Lodge began as a love story in May of 1989 at the University of Chicago. Mike and Jan met at a business conference on building a sense of community in the workplace. They met on the last day on the last shuttlebus back to the hotel. Mike's version of the story is a little more interesting than Jan's... In sharing what they would really like to do with their lives they both expressed their desire to run a retreat center. Their relationship grew long distance from Santa Fe, New Mexico to Hagerstown, Maryland, as they created a management development program, the Nature of Business. The foundation of the program was Nature and what it can teach us, personally and organizationally. The program required a Lodge environment – a great location surrounded by nature with comfortable accommodations, great food and warm hospitality. What they found were great nature locations (the likes of 4-H camps) and great accommodations (the likes of 4-star hotels) but nothing that had it all. Then the conversations began. "Why don't we just build it ourselves?"

With that simple question began the building of a dream. With their intentions set the impossible began to happen. Divine intervention? Perhaps. Divine stupidity? More probable. They didn't know they couldn't do it, so they did. That's how they explain it. "This is what we were brought together for – this is what we were intended to do with our lives. We have been blessed and directed. We had a vision and a dream. The naysayers said it couldn't be done and there were times we thought that maybe they might be right. But in the end we have done the impossible."

Build it and they will come... yes, a movie that inspired us, and also the truth of the matter. Once we said, "Let's build a Lodge", strange and wonderful things began to happen. The right people at the right time came into our lives. Not everything happened in our time frame, but in the right time frame. The dream was realized when our first guests stayed with us in October 1999.

"*Whatever you vividly imagine, ardently desire, sincerely believe, and enthusiastically act upon must inevitably come to pass*"

– Paul J. Meyer

Savage River Lodge

Savage River Lodge
1600 Mt. Aetna Road
Frostburg, Maryland 21532
Phone 301-689-3200
www.savageriverlodge.com

About Ravenwood Press

Launched in 2005, Ravenwood Press, Inc., publishes stories of Amazing Grace. Our books and calendars combine soul-stirring photography with insightful narrative to celebrate and honor the majesty of God's Creation. When divine grace flows through us, we are fully alive, sharing our gifts and talents to lift up others while making this world a better place. Ravenwood Press currently features the photography of Baltimore native Middleton Evans. While North American wildlife is a passionate interest, Mr. Evans has spent the majority of his 20-year career documenting the many faces of Maryland. Favorite subjects include Chesapeake Bay watermen, cities and towns, festivals, farm life and equestrian sports. A milestone was reached in 2001 when Maryland Public Television selected Mr. Evans as one of six local photographers to be featured in the documentary film *Images of Maryland: 1900 – 2000*, chronicling the state's most distinguished lensmen of the twentieth century. A 1982 graduate of McDonogh School, he began his professional career within a week of graduating from Duke University. Returning home from North Carolina with a degree in Economics, but no defined

photo by Jessica Earle

career path, he put his imagination to work. A life-long passion for photography, ignited by a semester abroad in London, was parlayed into a two-year photographic odyssey through Maryland, with hopes of being published. In 1988 a family business was launched to realize that dream, and *Maryland in Focus* was released to celebrate the compelling subjects encountered along his travels. Encouraged by rave reviews, Middleton next set his sights on Baltimore, capturing its colorful characters, charming neighborhoods, architectural icons, and vibrant cultural life. After *Baltimore* was published in 1992, a new challenge was sought, and the allure of nature photography beckoned. Four years of exploring roads less traveled culminated with *Maryland's Great Outdoors*, an inspiring collection of wildlife portraits, lush landscapes and outdoor adventures. In 1998 his career took yet another turn. An extraordinary 10-day Florida bird marathon served as the genesis of *Rhapsody in Blue*, an epic five-year adventure including 38 trips all over North America in search of miraculous encounters with native waterbirds. Over the same time frame Evans made hundreds of trips to his favorite pond in Baltimore's Patterson Park, better known for soccer games and summer concerts than Wood Ducks and Yellow-bellied Sapsuckers. An astounding 120 bird species, and many other natural treasures, were discovered in this urban oasis for a book to be titled *The Miracle Pond*, slated for a fall 2008 release. Ravenwood Press will be expanding its offerings in the near future with such projects as the amazing life and adventures of pioneering *National Geographic* photojournalist Thomas Abercrombie and his wife Lynn; the secret lives of wild tigers in India's Bandhavgarh National Park, by wildlife photographer Kim Sullivan; and Kristie Evans' children's books, including *Maxwell Smellswell and his Canine Capers*.

Rhapsody in Blue:
A Celebration of North American Waterbirds

Traveling to the continent's wild perimeter in search of glorious North American waterbirds... this was the adventure of a lifetime. Middleton Evans made 38 trips over a five-year period to complete his "wish list" of alluring species, captivating behaviors, and pristine habitats. A remarkable trip to Florida in 1998 inspired the project with ten days of daily surprises. On a wing and a prayer, Evans dropped his current Baltimore project and dreamed up shots to fill a unique coffee table book celebrating North America's waterbirds at their finest. God poured out blessings time and again, as the veil lifted to reveal profound moments. With absolute devotion toward the birds, they returned it tenfold to the camera.

Maryland's Great Outdoors

From the Appalachian Mountains to the Atlantic beaches, Maryland has earned the nickname "America in Miniature." A mere two hundred miles wide, this ninth smallest state is remarkably endowed with plant and animal life harbored in unique habitats. Wild orchids, carnivorous bog plants, mysterious forest creatures, regal birds of prey and dazzling butterflies... these are just some of the treasures encountered over four years of exploring Maryland's wild places. With nearly three hundred photographs, *Maryland's Great Outdoors* is a compelling collection that lifts the spirit with the glory and majesty of Creation.

THE BODHI CALENDAR
12 months of fun, fantasy, smiles
and a big scoop of nostalgia.

"Thank you for visiting my lodge. I hope that you enjoyed your stay. Y'all come back now real soon."

Thank You,
– Bodhi